RIVER WINDING

RIVER WINDING

poems by Charlotte Zolotow

pictures by Kazue Mizumura

A WORLD'S WORK CHILDREN'S BOOK

Other books by Charlotte Zolotow

Someone New
illustrated by Erik Blegvad

May I Visit?
illustrated by Erik Blegvad

It's Not Fair
illustrated by William Pène du Bois

My Grandson Lew
illustrated by William Pène du Bois

Big Sister, Little Sister
illustrated by Martha Alexander

Janey
illustrated by Ronald Himler

The Sky Was Blue
illustrated by Garth Williams

The Summer Night
illustrated by Ben Shecter

Wake Up and Good Night
illustrated by Leonard Weisgard

When the Wind Stops
illustrated by Howard Knotts

Text copyright © 1970 by Charlotte Zolotow
Illustrations copyright © 1978 by Kazue Mizumura
All rights reserved
First published in Great Britain 1980 by
World's Work Ltd
The Windmill Press
Kingswood, Tadworth, Surrey
Printed and bound in Great Britain by
Fakenham Press Limited, Fakenham, Norfolk

SBN 437 89514 9

To Grace C. and Steve Z.

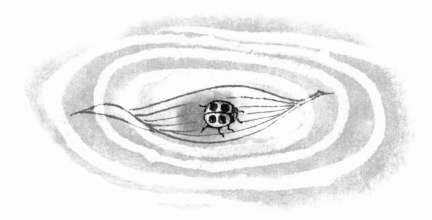

River Winding

Rain falling, what things do you grow?
Snow melting, where do you go?
Wind blowing, what trees do you know?
River winding, where do you flow?

The Spring Wind

The summer wind
is soft and sweet
the winter wind is strong
the autumn wind is mischievous
and sweeps the leaves along.

The wind I love the best
comes gently after rain
smelling of spring and growing things
brushing the world with feathery wings
while everything glistens, and everything sings
in the spring wind
after the rain.

Azalea

I feel as though
this bush were grown
especially for me.
I feel as though
I almost am
this little flowering tree.

Change

The summer
still hangs
heavy and sweet
with sunlight
as it did last year.

The autumn
still comes
showering gold and crimson
as it did last year.

The winter
still stings
clean and cold and white
as it did last year.

The spring
still comes
like a whisper in the dark night.

It is only I
who have changed.

The Wedding

I have been to a wedding
it was flowers and music and lace.
The bride was beautiful.
I knew her face
but the whiteness made her strange
and she didn't know me
though
I'm
her sister.

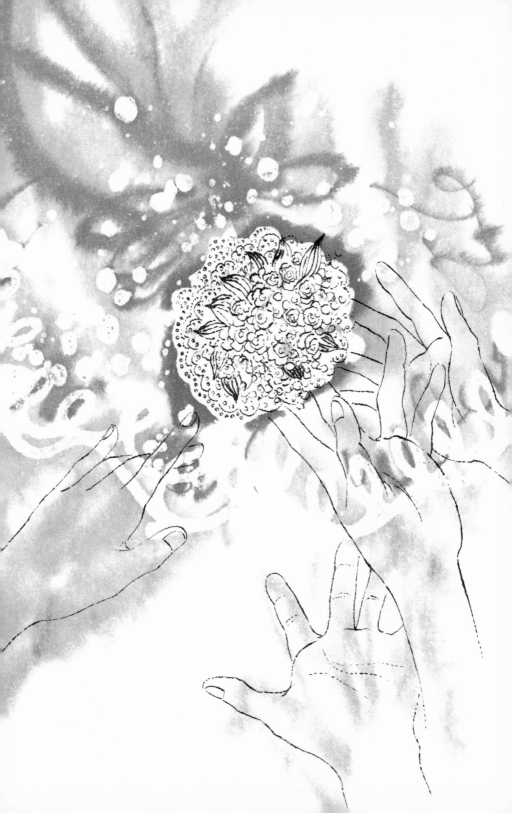

Little Bird

Little hurt bird
in my hand
your heart beats
like the pound of the sea
under the warmth
of your soft feathers.

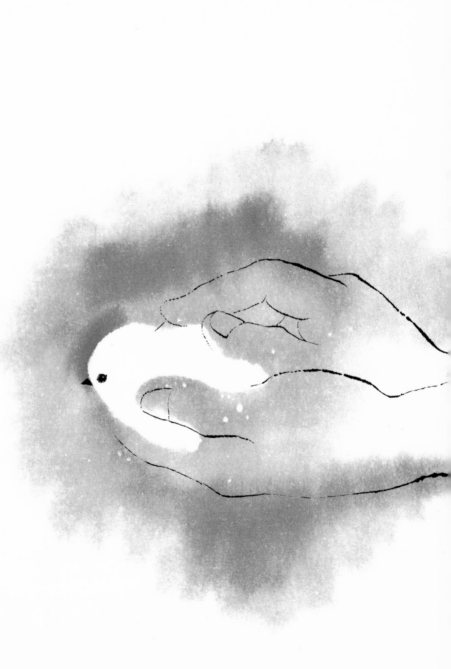

Autumn

Now the summer is grown old
the light long summer
                    is grown old.
Leaves change
and the garden is gold
with marigolds and zinnias
tangled and bold
blazing blazing
orange and gold.
                    The light long summer
                    is grown old.

The Cat

There is a cat prowling
through my garden
like a small tiger
looking for her prey.
But with a lovely flacking sound
all the birds
       fly away.

How Strange

How strange when I finally die
to lie beneath the grass and snow
while overhead the birds fly by
and I can't watch them go.

No One Would Believe

No one would believe
unless they saw too
as the train passed him
                    (but it's true)
facing the river
alone in the wind
an old old man
playing violin.

The Sandpiper

Look at the little sandpiper
skittering along the sandy shore
such a little light thing
such a little bright thing
stencilling tiny clawprints
waves will wash away
                    once more.

In Bed

When I am in bed
I hear
footsteps of the night
sharp
like the crackling of a dead leaf
in the stillness.

Then my mother laughs
downstairs.

A Dog

I am alone.
Someone is raking leaves
outside
and there is one yellow leaf
on the black branch
brushing the window.

Suddenly a wet cold nose
nuzzles
my empty hand.

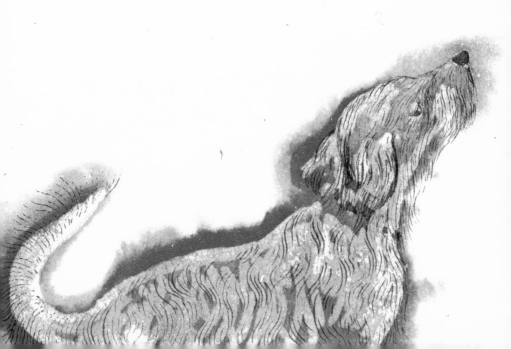

Missing You

Once we laughed together
by the river side
and watched the little waves
watched the waves.

Now I walk
along the bank
the water's very blue
and I am walking by the waves
walking by the waves
                    missing you.

River in Winter

The ice moves slowly
                    down the river
the gulls
          are circling
                    high
grey and white
grey and white
against
          the
                grey-blue
                        sky!

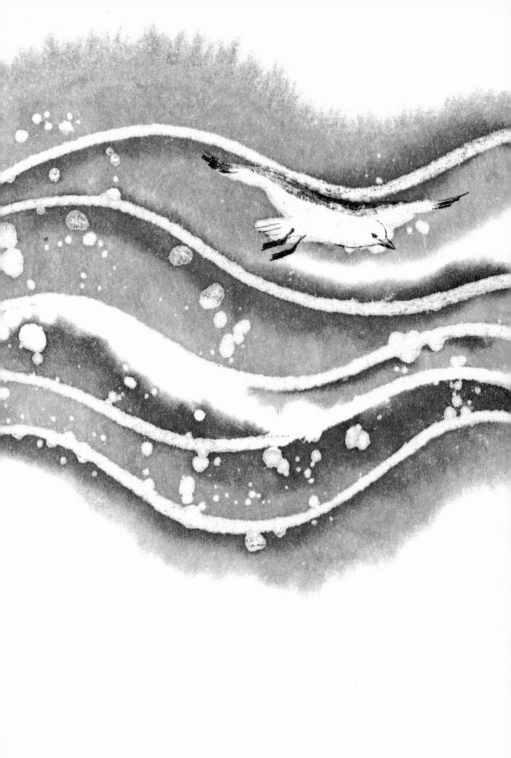

Little Old Man

Little old man hunched and grey
I know you were young once—like me.
But it's hard to believe I'll ever be
the way I see you are today
hunched and grey
little old man
(once young like me)

A Moment in Summer

A moment in summer
belongs to me
and one particular
honey bee.
A moment in summer
shimmering clear
making the sky
seem very near,
a moment in summer
belongs to me.

Violets

Someone is coming
down the road
and they may buy
a bunch of our violets
purple and sweet
smelling of spring.
But we won't tell
the secret place
where they grow.
No one will know
the tall grass
where we found them.
No one can buy
the feeling of the hot sun
on our hair
as we picked them.
It is only the flowers themselves
the violets
purple and sweet
they'll take away.

Scene

Little trees like pencil strokes
black and still
etched forever in my mind
on that snowy hill.

Reflection

Reflection in the water
upside down
if I really reached you
I would drown.

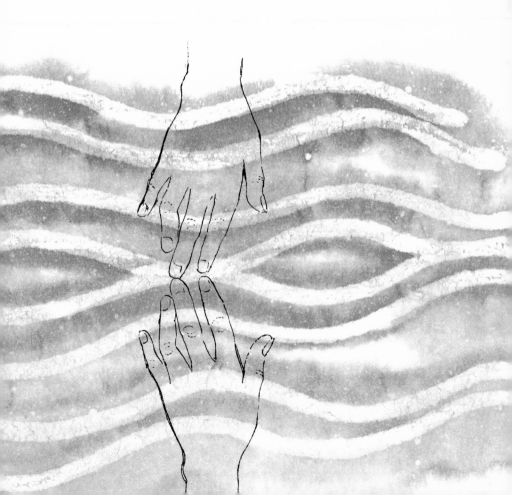

So Will I

My grandfather remembers long ago
the white Queen Anne's lace that grew wild.
He remembers the buttercups and goldenrod
from when he was a child.

He remembers long ago
the white snow falling falling.
He remembers the bluebird and thrush
at twilight
calling, calling.

He remembers long ago
the new moon in the summer sky
He remembers the wind in the trees
and its long, rising sigh.
And so will I
              so will I.

Bedtime

the day is over
the night comes gently
the bathtub water
                is green and warm

the little girl comes down the stairs
gaily
shining from her bath
like a Christmas ball

the fire dances for her
like a princess swaying swaying

and her mother when she kisses her good night
is soft
with pillow smell

she hears the wind ruffling outside
saying sleep sleep sleep